Logic Puzzles
to Bend
your Brain

Kurt Smith

Sterling Publishing Co., Inc.
New York

Dedicated to my co-conspirator,
my smashing editor in chief,
my wonderful wife, my best friend,
Martha.

Library of Congress Cataloging-in-Publication Data Available

10   9   8

Published by Sterling Publishing Co., Inc.
387 Park Avenue South, New York, NY 10016
© 2003 by Kurt Smith
Distributed in Canada by Sterling Publishing
℅ Canadian Manda Group, 165 Dufferin Street
Toronto, Ontario, Canada M6K 3H6
Distributed in Great Britain and Europe by Chris Lloyd at Orca Book
Services, Stanley House, Fleets Lane, Poole BH15 3AJ, England
Distributed in Australia by Capricorn Link (Australia) Pty. Ltd.
P.O. Box 704, Windsor, NSW 2756, Australia

Sterling ISBN 0-8069-8012-5

For information about custom editions, special sales, premium and
corporate purchases, please contact Sterling Special Sales
Department at 800-805-5489 or specialsales@sterlingpub.com.

CONTENTS

Brainbender Puzzles 4

At the Zoo

Five animals at the zoo get into an argument about their ages because the oldest gets fed first and they're all ravenous. See if you can figure out how old each animal is.

1. The otter is older than the leopard.
2. The emu is younger than the otter.
3. The leopard is older than the hippopotamus.
4. The hippo is older than the emu and the lion.
5. The lion is older than the emu.

	10	11	12	13	14
emu					
hippo					
leopard					
lion					
otter					

See answers on page 80.

Stephanie's Water Bottle

Stephanie brought a filled water bottle to class. Several of her students wanted a drink from it, so Stephanie got paper cups and offered some. The first person, Teresa, took 1/4 of the total. Brady then took 1/5 of what remained. After that, Keith took 1/3 of what was left. The next person, Cathy, took 1/2 of what was remaining. Kent then took two ounces, leaving Stephanie with the remaining two ounces. How many ounces of water did Stephanie start with?

See answer on page 91.

Cornivores

In Tristan's Video Arcade, the Corn Eaters from the *Cornivores* game got out and started eating some of the creatures from the other games. When Tristan opened his arcade the next morning he discovered, to his horror, that several creatures were missing. Using these excellent clues, figure out exactly how many of each kind are missing and which games they belong in.

1. There were 21 more Grabbers taken than Wombats.
2. A total of 115 creatures were eaten in the night.
3. Some of the Iguanidae from Lizard Lair were eaten, about 10 fewer than the Trocta from the Trout School.
4. All of the Wombats are gone! There were 11. Poor little fuzzy critters.
5. 44 Loon Goons are gone.

Wombat Willies	Lagoon Slimeballs	Trout School	Body Grabbers	Lizard Lair

See answers on page 82.

WAIT! In an unexpected turn of events, the *Cornivore* denizens admitted that all the creatures were simply creature-napped, not eaten, and they have all been returned to their games. Whew! That was a close one, eh, Tristan?

A Man in a Green Coat

Five people put a gallon of gasoline in their vehicles to see who could go the farthest. Using the clues, including the conversion information below, figure out which vehicle went farthest, who drove it, and what color it was.

1 mile (mi.) = 1.6 kilometers (k.)

1. The red motorcycle traveled 12 k. farther than the SUV.
2. One vehicle, not the SUV, went 34.5 miles.
3. The old woman drove 55.2 k.
4. The person driving the motorcycle wore a green coat and traveled 48 k.
5. The referee traveled 19.2 k. fewer than the one in tennis shoes and 4.5 mi. fewer than the green station wagon.
6. The one in ski boots traveled 27 miles per gallon.
7. The driver of the blue sports car wore gold earrings.
8. The orange vehicle traveled 22.5 miles.
9. The five vehicles traveled a total of 150 miles.

See answers on page 87.

	station wagon	motorcycle	SUV	pickup	sports car	k.	mi.
man in green coat							
woman with gold earrings							
teen in ski boots							
old woman in tennis shoes							
basketball referee							
blue							
black							
green							
red							
orange							
k.							
mi.							

Vanilla Swirl

How much ice cream could you eat in five minutes? Six kids had a little contest to see who could eat the most. They all went to Leo's Ice Cream Palace and told Leo to "bring it on," meaning, of course, to serve them a lot of ice cream. See if you can figure out who ate the most, how much, and what kind. Have fun dreaming of being in a contest like this!

1. Sara ate half as many scoops as Caleb.
2. Neither Joey nor Loren likes raspberry.
3. Joey ate fewer scoops than Sydney.
4. The one who ate peach ice cream won the contest.
5. Dakota doesn't like rocky road.
6. Loren ate more than twice as much as Sara.
7. The one who ate four scoops chose vanilla swirl.
8. Sydney, who chose rocky road, ate three more scoops than Joey.
9. Loren ate three more scoops than Dakota.
10. Sydney ate two fewer scoops than Loren.
11. The one who chose chocolate ate two more scoops than the one who chose vanilla swirl.

See answers on page 92.

	Scoops						strawberry	raspberry	vanilla swirl	peach	rocky road	chocolate
	2	3	4	5	6	7						
Caleb												
Dakota												
Joey												
Sara												
Loren												
Sydney												
2							
3							
4							
5							
6							
7							
strawberry							
raspberry							
vanilla swirl							
peach							
rocky road							
chocolate							

Scoops

Beverly's Yard Sale

Beverly decided to have a yard sale to get rid of a bunch of yards—and some feet and inches, too—that had been piling up in her den. She advertised this way:

Yard Sale

Yards and other assorted lengths.

MUST GO!   **Cheap!**

By noon she had sold almost everything. Just a few items were left, all of which Beverly plans to send to be recycled. Using the following information, figure out how much Beverly made on her yard sale and how many feet she will donate to recycling.

Started With	Sold	Cost Price	Earned	Left Over (in feet)
13 yards	11 yards	.20 per foot		
27 feet	8 yards	.03 per inch		
216 inches	186 inches	.24 per foot		
		Total Earned		
		Recycled		

See answers on page 81.

The Great Divide

Four boys have three candy bars—a Snickers, a Hershey's chocolate bar, and a Mars. They agreed to cut one bar into three pieces, one into four pieces, and one into five pieces. They then took turns (how mature of them!) and each one got to pick one piece of a bar of their choice until everyone had three pieces. With the clues below, figure out who got which pieces and each of their last names.

1. Smith did not select a Mars piece.
2. Jeremy took two of the four Mars pieces, but no Hershey's.
3. Jones was the only one who did not get a piece of Snickers.
4. Derek and Smith each had one more Hershey's than Tyler.
5. Jason took no Mars pieces.
6. Greene took no Hershey's.
7. Ozzie took one Mars piece.

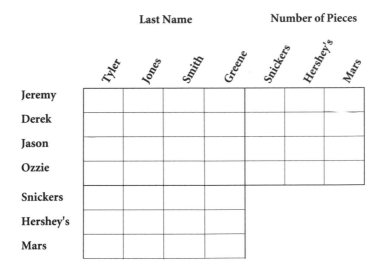

See answers on page 85.

Paper Clips

A total of 303 whole paper clips are in 12 boxes. The box with the fewest has four. Another box has 39. Based on the following, how many paper clips are in each box?

Box C contains half as many as Box J.
Box F contains 1/10 as many as Box D.
Box L contains 1/5 as many as Box E.
Box H contains five times more than Box F.
Box L contains two fewer than Box C.
Box I contains three times as many as Box C.
Box A contains half as many as Box K.
Box K contains one fewer than Box I.
Box B contains four times as many as Box F.
Box G contains twice that of Box L.

A	B	C	D	E	F

G	H	I	J	K	L

See answers on page 90.

Four Football Fans and Four Pizzas

Four guys are watching a football game. Four frozen pizzas are waiting in the freezer. By the end of the first quarter, all four pizzas are ready to eat. (Yes, they did cook them first.) Because not all the guys like the same kind, they slice the four pizzas this way:

3 pepperoni pizza slices
5 cheese pizza slices
4 sausage pizza slices
4 vegetarian pizza slices

Using the clues below, answer these questions: Which guy ate which kinds of pizza, and how many slices of each? Note: All four guys had four slices.

1. No one ate more than three slices of any one kind.
2. $1/16$ of the pizza slices, a pepperoni one, was chosen by Hank. Another $1/16$ that he had was vegetarian.
3. $3/16$ of Peter's choices were just one kind. $1/16$ was vegetarian.
4. Two of the guys ate one of each kind.
5. Jason does not like cheese pizza.

	pepperoni slices			cheese slices			sausage slices			vegetarian slices		
	1	2	3	1	2	3	1	2	3	1	2	3
Peter												
Bob												
Hank												
Jason												

See answers on page 84.

Babysitting

Five young people have been babysitting to earn extra money. Each one is saving for something special. Using the clues given, figure out how much each makes per hour, how much each has earned so far, and what each is saving to buy.

1. Dylan has earned the most so far, although he makes the least per hour.
2. Carson has worked 19 hours, 23 fewer than Wills.
3. Gray makes $4.75 and has worked 35 hours so far. She's saving for the bicycle.
4. The person saving for a computer (not Amelia or Ellis) earns $5.25 per hour and has earned $99.75 so far.
5. The one saving for the clothes is neither Elvin nor Jones.
6. Sands has worked 66 hours so far.
7. The person saving for college has worked 38 hours so far; the one saving for clothes has worked 42.

See answers on page 80.

	Last Name					$ Earned So Far					$ per Hour				
	Wills	Sands	Jones	Ellis	Gray	264.00	166.25	99.75	189.00	190.00	4.00	4.50	4.75	5.00	5.25
Amelia															
Bobby															
Carson															
Dylan															
Elvin															
trip															
bicycle															
computer															
college															
clothes															
$4.00															
$4.50															
$4.75															
$5.00															
$5.25															

Berry Streets Bus

The last five students to get off the school bus in the afternoon are Diana, Bruce, Tracy, Danny, and Justin. Each lives on the street where he or she leaves the bus. Using these six clues, determine the order the students get off the bus and the street each lives on.

1. Danny gets off the bus before Justin and Tracy; Justin leaves before Diana.
2. Huckleberry Avenue is between Cherry Street and Elderberry Road.
3. Tracy leaves the bus after Bruce.
4. The name of the second person off the bus doesn't begin with "D".
5. Diana gets off the bus between Huckleberry and Mulberry Street, both of which are before Blueberry Street.
6. The person who gets off the bus next to last lives between Elderberry and Blueberry.

	Diana	Bruce	Tracy	Danny	Justin
Mulberry					
Blueberry					
Huckleberry					
Cherry					
Elderberry					
1st					
2nd					
3rd					
4th					
5th					

Leaves Bus (row label for 1st–5th)

See answers on page 80.

Check!

Bob and Al play a lot of chess. Because Al is better than Bob, when they decided to play a 5-day marathon match they agreed to the following point system:

	Checkmates	Draws	Stalemates
Bob	3.5 points	¾ point	¼ point
Al	1.5 points	½ point	⅛ point

Who won this marathon of 48 games? (Try doing this one without using a calculator!)

	Checkmates	Draws	Stalemates	Total
Bob	11	8	2	
Al	27	8	2	

See answers on page 82.

My Favorite Class

Eighty students were surveyed about their favorite class. Using this pie chart, record the responses of the correct number of students (round off to nearest whole number).

_____ English

_____ PE

_____ Social Studies

_____ Art

_____ Math

_____ Biology

Math 6%
Art 13%
Biology 10%
PE 31%
Social Studies 25%
English 15%

See answers on page 89.

Hogs in a Fog

Five hog farmers were taking their hogs to the Annual County Fair when a sudden fog came up at an intersection at exactly the time all five were crossing, causing everyone to run into each other. No one was injured, but all the hogs—a total of 336—got loose and ran into the fog. From the clues, how many hogs were in each truck?

1. The Dodge carried four times as many hogs as the Chevrolet.
2. The largest load, 1/3 of the hogs, had been in the Mack.
3. The smallest load, 24 hogs, was not from the Ford.
4. The Ford carried 24 fewer hogs than the GMC.

Chevrolet	Dodge	Ford	GMC	Mack

See answers on page 85.

Mr. Clark's PE Storage Room

Mr. Clark cleaned out his PE room the other day and found a mess of balls he'd thought were lost. How many balls did he find?

1. Six more tetherballs than footballs.
2. Fewer footballs than soccer balls.
3. Half as many soccer balls as softballs.

	4	8	10	12	16
basketballs					
soccer balls					
softballs					
footballs					
tetherballs					

See answers on page 88.

Sit-ups

These guys are crazy! About sit-ups, that is. Every morning before school they meet in the gym for a sit-up race. This morning, how many sit-ups did each boy do?

1. Logan did half as many as Leo.
2. Nicky did twice as many as Zack.
3. Chan did ⅓ as many as Axel.
4. Dale did three times more than Andy.
5. Leo did half as many as Dale.
6. Chan did three times as many as Zack.
7. Andy did ⅔ as many as Leo.
8. Logan did three times more than Nicky.
9. The fewest number of sit-ups was five.
10. One of the boys did 60.

_____ Andy   _____ Chan   _____ Nicky   _____ Leo

_____ Axel   _____ Dale   _____ Logan   _____ Zack

See answers on page 90.

Wholesome Decimals

By adding or subtracting the decimals inside the box, create seven whole numbers. *Hints: Don't mix operations in the same problem, and use each number only once.*

6.09	.25	3.96
5.47	7.997	.22
9.25	4.78	.003
.91	.04	.878
.53	.121	.001

See answers on page 93.

Bobcats

The Bobcats basketball team is very good. They shoot like crazy and are great rebounders. Using all the clues below, see if you can determine the full name of each Bobcat varsity player, how tall each is, and their scoring averages.

1. Jon is not the tallest, but he's taller than Aaron.
2. Ben and Lien are the two shortest.
3. Blum played in 12 games and scored a total of 228 points.
4. Dan is taller than Delg, who is taller than Ross.
5. The one who scored 132 in 15 games is not Katz or Sid.
6. Ben is 3" shorter than Sid.
7. Ross, who scored a total of 219 points in 15 games, is 6'3".
8. The shortest player does not have the lowest shooting average.
9. Delg is 7" taller than Lien.
10. The tallest player has the highest average.

See answers on page 81.

| | Last Name | | | | | Height | | | | | Scoring Average | | | | |
---	Blum	Ross	Delg	Katz	Lien	5'9"	6'0"	6'3"	6'7"	6'9"	4.5	8.0	8.8	14.6	19.0
Aaron															
Ben															
Dan															
Sid															
Jon															
4.5															
8.0															
8.8															
14.6															
19.0															
5'9"															
6'0"															
6'3"															
6'7"															
6'9"															

Misplaced Numbers

It seems that a number of numbers have been misplaced. Your task is to put them all back in their correct boxes, *in order from lowest to highest,* according to these rules:

Box A: Even numbers larger than 12.
Box B: Odd numbers smaller than 40.
Box C: The products of numbers multiplied by 9.
Box D: The products of numbers multiplied by 7.
Box E: All other numbers.

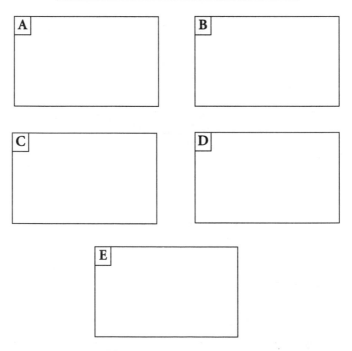

Misplaced Numbers: 45, 57, 73, 13, 87, 10, 20, 1, 117, 26, 95, 8, 105, 38, 19, 49, 135, 2, 16, 99, 91, 83, 59

A

B

C

D

E

See answers on page 88.

Corn Dogs

Dwight sells corn dogs, pretzels, peanuts, and popcorn at baseball games. Today he sold everything he had. How much did he sell?

1. Four times as many hot dogs as popcorn.
2. More corn dogs than pretzels and popcorn combined.
3. Three times more peanuts than popcorn.

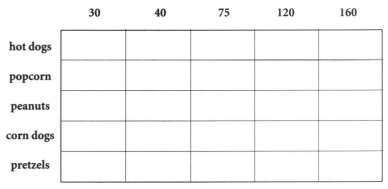

	30	40	75	120	160
hot dogs					
popcorn					
peanuts					
corn dogs					
pretzels					

See answers on page 82.

Five Boxes

1. Each box has a whole number in it.
2. The number in Box A is 12 times larger than Box B.
3. Box D is ½ as large as Box A, and is the product of Boxes B and C.
4. Box E, containing the middle-sized number, is the sum of Box C and another box.
5. Box C is Box A divided by eight.
6. One of the boxes contains the number four.

A	B	C	D	E

See answers on page 83.

Magazine Drive

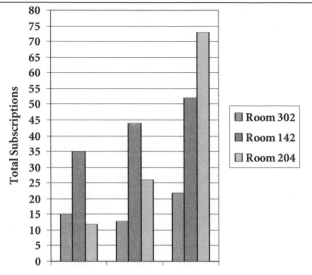

1. Room _____ sold twice as many subscriptions in November as Room _____ did in December.
2. In October, total sales were _____.
3. The best selling month was _____, with _____ subscriptions.
4. The best selling room was _____, with _____ subscriptions.
5. Room _____ sold twice as many subscriptions in November as Room _____.
6. Total sales for the month of _____ were more than the other two months combined.
7. Room _____ sold eight more subscriptions than the other two combined in the month of _____.
8. The largest difference in sales occurred in the month of _____, between Room _____ and Room _____.
9. Only Room _____ failed to make a gain each month.
10. Room _____ made the biggest gain, from _____ in the month of _____ to _____ in the month of _____.

See answers on page 87.

Dale's Trip

Dale took a little time off from his deli to do some traveling. He traveled in his car through a foreign country in which gas stations sold gas by the liter. Using the conversion table and the clues I give you, see if you can tell how much gas he used both in gallons and liters, the average he paid for the gas, and how many miles he went per gallon.

Conversion Chart	
Gallons	Liters
1	3.79

Dale set his trip indicator at zero and filled his car with 53.06 liters of gas at $1.90 per gallon. He traveled 210 miles and added 5 gallons at a place that sold it for $1.99. The next stop he filled up again for $1.89 and it took 45.48 liters after traveling 225 miles. The next time he needed gas he had driven 199 miles and put in 9 gallons at a price of $1.78 each. His last stop was after driving 230 miles at a place that sold gas for $2.09, and he needed 41.69 liters.

total gallons

total liters

average $ per gallon

miles per gallon

See answers on page 82.

Halloween Party

IT'S A PARTY! Candy. Cider. Costumes. Tons of sugar. You know the drill. Anyway, figure out who wore the witch's costume, who won the pumpkin-carving contest, who won the apple-bobbing contest, how many glasses of cider each drank, who got sick (yuk!), who broke their mother's dish in the apple-bobbing bucket, and who helped the teacher clean up afterward.

1. The one who broke the dish drank three glasses of cider.
2. Emily drank two more glasses of cider than Katie.
3. The one who wore the witch's costume drank six glasses of cider.
4. The one who helped clean up after drank four glasses of cider.
5. The one who drank one glass of cider won the pumpkin-carving contest.
6. Sam drank half as many glasses of cider as Emily.
7. Donny drank three more glasses of cider than Erin.
8. The person who got sick drank two glasses of cider. (I guess she didn't like it that much.)
9. The one who wore the witch's costume (not Donny) drank five more glasses of cider than Dina.

See answers on page 85.

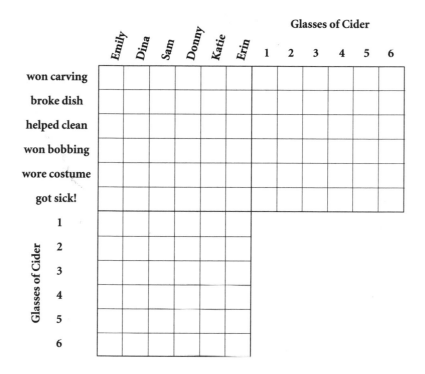

Martha's Books

Martha loves books! She has books all over the place...on her bookshelves, on the windowsill, under her bed, on shelves in the dining room, in the hallway, in closets. Her mother asked her to put some of her books into five boxes. Using these clues, figure out how many books she put into each box. *Hint: There are actually two different answers to this one, both correct!*

1. Martha was able to stuff 180 books into the five boxes.
2. The box with the most books has 12 more than the second largest.
3. The box with the fewest books, not A or D, has $1/15$ of the total number of books.
4. Box D has twice as many books as B.
5. $\frac{1}{3}$ of the books are in one of the boxes.
6. Box C has 24 fewer books than E.

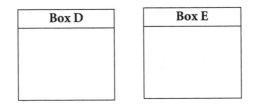

See answers on page 87.

The Dalton Express

Poor Engineer Jones... He lost his train schedule! Seems it must have fallen out of his engineer's vest pocket while he was having an espresso at Half-Off Dale's Deli. All he remembers is that he leaves Dalton at 7:15 this morning, stops at several cities on the way to Reedville, then comes back to Dalton, nonstop, at the end of the day. From years of experience, he knows that the train waits exactly six minutes from the time it arrives at each station until it departs. He also knows that the train averages 48 miles per hour during the trip to Reedville and 56 miles per hour on the nonstop trip back to Dalton. Can you help him recreate his schedule?

Mileage from Dalton	
Carroll	96
Farmington	12
Newton	24
Portsmouth	156
Reedville	168

City	Arrive	Depart
Dalton	—	7:15
Farmington		
Newton		
Carroll		
Portsmouth		
Reedville		
Dalton		—

See answers on page 82.

Double Bogey

Eagle	= 2 strokes under par
Birdie	= 1 stroke under par
Par	= same score as the scorecard
Bogey	= 1 stroke over par
Double Bogey	= two strokes over par

Four friends played nine holes of golf. They all shot par on each hole except the following. What were their scores?

Hole 1: Smith had an eagle, Munro had a double bogey, and Dyment had a birdie.

Hole 2: Horn had a bogey, Munro had a birdie.

Hole 3: Smith had a birdie, Dyment had a double bogey, Horn had a bogey.

Hole 4: Munro had a birdie.

Hole 5: Dyment had a double bogey, Smith had a birdie, Horn had an eagle.

Hole 6: Horn had a double bogey, Smith had a birdie, Munro had a bogey.

Hole 7: Smith had another eagle, Horn had a birdie, Dyment had a bogey.

Hole 8: Munro had a birdie.

Hole 9: Dyment had a birdie, Horn had a double bogey, Smith had a bogey.

Scorecard

Par	4	5	3	4	4	3	5	4	4	36
Hole	1	2	3	4	5	6	7	8	9	Total
Smith										
Dyment										
Horn										
Munro										

See answers on page 83.

Warm-ups

Mr. Clark is at it again—pushing his students to work hard! Use this chart to determine how many points each student earned in PE class during warm-ups.

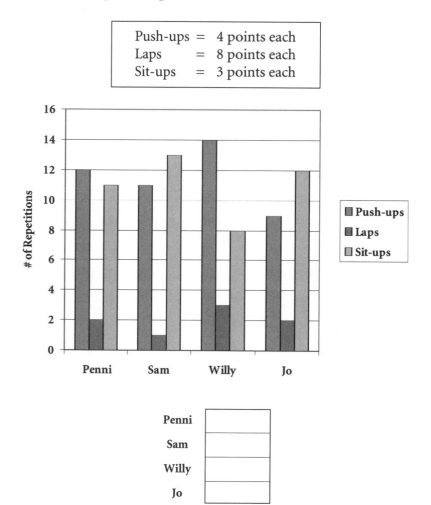

Push-ups = 4 points each
Laps   = 8 points each
Sit-ups = 3 points each

See answers on page 93.

Odometer

Five people drove their cars from Seattle to Portland, a distance of 185 miles. To check the accuracy of their odometers, they each set their mileage indicators to zero in a parking lot at Safeco Field. They each drive a different colored car. Using the excellent clues I'm going to offer, figure out the full names of all the drivers, the colors of the cars they drive, and the reading of their odometers as they cross the I-5 bridge into Portland three hours later.

1. Shepard is not Roberta, nor is his car green.
2. The driver of the tan car is not Lester or Danny.
3. The odometer of the white car reads 6.9 miles fewer than the black car.
4. Rudy is neither Fisher nor Delphino.
5. The car driven by Swank is tan and the mileage is 2.2 more than Delphino's black car.
6. Lester's green car has 5.8 more miles than Roberta's red one.
7. Willy's tan car has .8 more miles than Curley's.

See answers on page 89.

	Swank	Shepard	Fisher	Lester	Delphino	179.4	181.9	186.3	187.7	188.5
Curley										
Roberta										
Rudy										
Willy										
Danny										
green										
red										
black										
tan										
white										
179.4										
181.9										
186.3										
187.7										
188.5										

Fraction Match

Your job here is to match the pictures with the fractions (put the letters of the matching pictures in the spaces at the bottom).

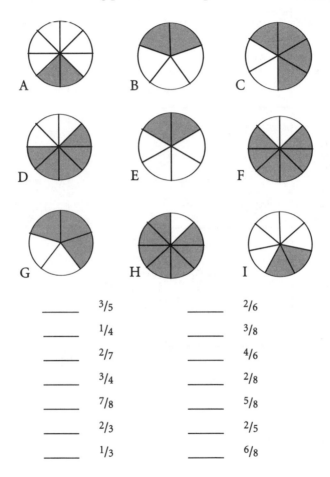

_____	$3/5$	_____	$2/6$
_____	$1/4$	_____	$3/8$
_____	$2/7$	_____	$4/6$
_____	$3/4$	_____	$2/8$
_____	$7/8$	_____	$5/8$
_____	$2/3$	_____	$2/5$
_____	$1/3$	_____	$6/8$

See answers on page 84.

Big hint #1: There is more than one answer for some of the pictures.
Big hint #2: There is one answer that has no picture representing it.
Draw a circle around it.

Paul's Guppies

Paul had a bowl of guppies for sale. Four customers were milling around in his store.

1. Rod told Paul, "I'll take half of the guppies in the bowl, plus half a guppy."
2. Heather, the second customer, said, "I'll take half of what you have left, plus half a guppy."
3. The third customer, Nancy, said, "I'll take half of what you have left, plus half a guppy."
4. Michele, the fourth customer, said, "I'll take half of what you have left, plus half a guppy."

All four of the customers left the store with live guppies, and Paul was happy to have sold all his fish. How many guppies were there in the bowl when he started? How many did each customer take?

customer	guppies bought
Rod	
Heather	
Nancy	
Michele	
total in bowl	

See answers on page 90.

Half-Off Dale's Deli

Dale offers his customers a half-order of any item on his menu (except drinks) for 40% off. Seven people just walked into Dale's Deli and ordered from this menu:

Hungarian Mushroom Soup	$3.00
Black Forest Ham Sandwich	$6.00
Roast Beef Sandwich	$6.00
Smoked Turkey Sandwich	$6.00
Chili	$2.50
Tuna Sandwich	$5.50
Cinnamon Roll	$2.00
Espresso	$2.25
All soft drinks	$1.25

Using the following clues, figure out what each person had for lunch, how much it cost, and who got stuck with the bill.

1. No one ordered both espresso and a soft drink, and no two people ordered the same kind of sandwich.
2. Neither Ginger, C.J., nor Beverly ordered a sandwich.
3. Three people ordered the mushroom soup; two of them ordered ½ a bowl.

	Sandwich		Soup		Chili	
	full	½	full	½	full	½
Ted						
Geri						
Ginger						
Kelsey						
Tristan						
Beverly						
C.J.						

See answers on page 85.

4. Kelsey ordered four items totaling $7.85. Her food items were ½ orders.
5. C.J. and Ginger later figured that if they had split a cinnamon roll instead of ordering two halves they'd have saved money. Neither of them had anything but the ½ cinnamon roll.
6. Three people ordered soft drinks (not Geri), and two ordered espressos (not Ted).
7. Tristan's lunch cost $11.25. He was the only one to have a full bowl of chili.
8. Four people ordered sandwiches: one was Tristan's tuna, and two were ½ orders.
9. Geri had four items including half a sandwich and half a bowl of chili. Her total was $9.35.
10. Ted, Tristan, and Kelsey each had a soft drink.
11. The one who paid the total bill of $47.15 (not Beverly or Ted) had four items including a bowl of chili and a soft drink.
12. Ted was the only one who didn't have a cinnamon roll. Not smart, Ted!
13. Just two people had chili and just two had espresso. One of the people had both.
14. Beverly ordered three items, including a full bowl of soup. Her total was $7.25.

Cinnamon Roll		Espresso	Soft Drinks	Lunch Cost
full	½			
			Total	
			Paid by	

B-r-r-r-r-r

Using the chart, answer the following (to the nearest tenth):

1. The average temperature for the week was _____ degrees.
2. The coldest day was below the average by _____ degrees.
3. The warmest day was above the average by _____ degrees.
4. The day closest to the average temperature was

   _____.
5. The biggest change from one day to the next was _____
   degrees.
6. On three different days, the temperature was the same: _____
   degrees.
7. It was (warmer / colder) on the weekend than the rest of the
   week. By how much (average)? _____.

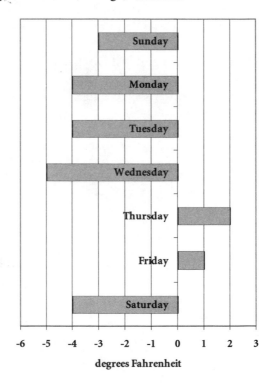

degrees Fahrenheit

See answers on page 81.

Kids and Cars

The kids in Mrs. Flapdoodle's class were asked what kind of car they would buy if they were old enough. Twenty-two kids filled out the survey. To the nearest whole number, how many chose which kind of car?

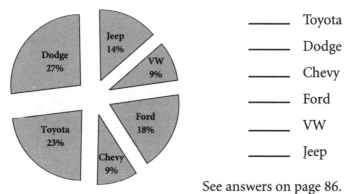

_____ Toyota

_____ Dodge

_____ Chevy

_____ Ford

_____ VW

_____ Jeep

See answers on page 86.

Farmer Bob's Barn

Bob sent Little Bob out to the barn one night to count the animals there. Can you figure out the numbers with just three clues?

1. Twice as many cows as horses.
2. Two more chickens than goats.
3. Six more goats than horses.

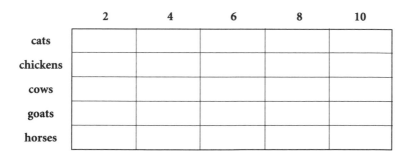

	2	4	6	8	10
cats					
chickens					
cows					
goats					
horses					

See answers on page 83.

Jessica

Jessica got a new computer and she's driving her friends crazy with her questions. She charts the information she gets from them on her computer. Using her latest graph derived from birth dates, fill in the blanks below.

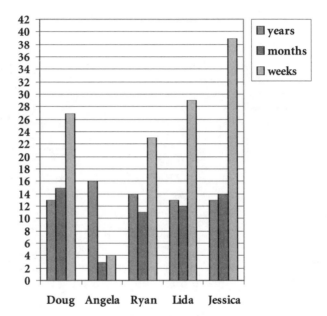

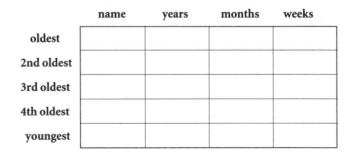

	name	years	months	weeks
oldest				
2nd oldest				
3rd oldest				
4th oldest				
youngest				

See answers on page 86.

Woody's Tires

A temperature change put the tire pressure in Woody's car out of whack. A tire place he went to uses gauges with kPa (kilopascals) rather than psi (pounds per square inch). To find kPA when you have psi, you have to multiply psi by 6.89. Woody is ready to either put air in his tires or let some out. Can you tell him how much?

	current tire pressure	desired pressure	add kPa's	subtract kPa's
right front	166.30 kPa	26 psi		
left front	184.98 kPa	26 psi		
right rear	199.32 kPa	28 psi		
left rear	147.86 kPa	28 psi		
spare	213.44	30 psi		

See answers on page 94.

Bogmen

As holidays approach, cranberry bogs are busy places as pounds of berries are shipped all over. Which bog shipped the most?

1. Miles o' Bogs shipped one-fifth more berries than Billy's Berries.
2. Grand Cranberries Ltd. shipped twice the amount of berries than Cranberries, Inc. did.
3. Tiny's Bog Co. shipped a third as many pounds as Grand Cranberries Ltd.

Pounds of Cranberries

	600	900	1,200	1,500	1,800	2,100
Billy's Berries						
Grand Cranberries Ltd.						
Tiny's Bog Co.						
Bog by the Bay						
Cranberries, Inc.						
Miles o' Bogs						

See answers on page 81.

Kookaburra Stew

Four kookaburras are planning a stew for dinner. Each one likes different ingredients. Using these delicious clues, determine which ingredient each kookaburra prefers and how much of it. Also, figure out the name of each bird, and where each is from.

Conversion Chart	
1 pint	= .47 liters
1 quart	= .94 liters
1 gallon	= 3.76 liters

1. The stew calls for a pint more scampi than perch.
2. The kookaburra from Wollongong prefers sardines.
3. The kookaburra from Wagga Wagga prefers scampi.
4. The recipe calls for 1.175 liters more perch than angleworm.
5. The kookaburra that likes angleworm in his stew is from Kangaroo Island.
6. Plato likes perch.
7. Neither the bird from Wollongong, nor Augustus, prefers angleworm. They eat it on occasion, but it's not their first choice.
8. The kookaburra from Wollongong recommends 2.585 liters more of his ingredient than Caesar does of his.

See answers on page 86.

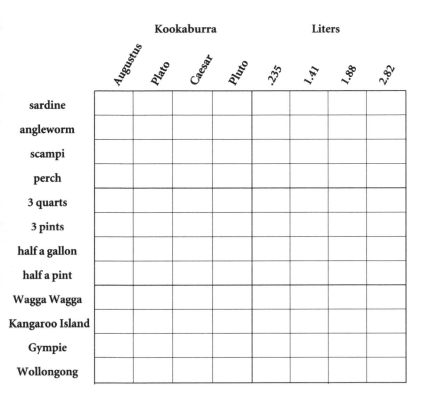

	Kookaburra				Liters			
	Augustus	Plato	Caesar	Pluto	.235	1.41	1.88	2.82
sardine								
angleworm								
scampi								
perch								
3 quarts								
3 pints								
half a gallon								
half a pint								
Wagga Wagga								
Kangaroo Island								
Gympie								
Wollongong								

Mr. Lockety's New Carpet

Four classrooms in Old Stewball School are getting new carpet, and Mr. Lockety is in charge. But, dashing to class, he lost all his requests. He's even forgotten what he needs in his own room! Which teacher gets which color, and how many square feet of carpet is needed for each? All measurements are in feet—no inches.

1. Room 168 is square.
2. Mrs. Eddy does not like sage.
3. Mr. Lockety's room is 27 feet long.
4. One of the dimensions of the room getting navy is 25 feet.
5. Mrs. Ebuley's room, 22 feet wide, will not have taupe carpet.
6. Just two rooms, taupe and 194, have one foot difference between length and width.
7. Room 186 (not mauve) is 22 feet wide.
8. Ms. Stalk isn't fond of taupe.

See answers on page 88.

	168	186	193	194	506	552	594	625	navy	mauve	taupe	sage
Mr. Lockety												
Mrs. Ebuley												
Ms. Stalk												
Mrs. Eddy												
506												
552												
594												
625												
navy												
mauve												
taupe												
sage												

Catapult

Four kittens weigh four pounds together, but they don't weigh one pound each. No, no, that would make this puzzle too easy for such a smart person as you. Two of the kittens weigh less than a pound and two of them weigh more than a pound. Four kids come along and take the four kittens. Makes sense, the kittens being really cute and all. So see if you can figure out which kid takes which kitten and how much each one weighs (no, not the kids…the kittens).

1. Catapult weighs more than the kitten taken by Martha.
2. The kitten that weighs 17 oz. is not Bandit.
3. Codi weighs just under a pound but is not the lightest.
4. Kurt's kitten is not Bandit.
5. Ted's kitten is not the largest, but weighs over a pound.
6. Hallie weighs less than Codi.
7. Martha's kitten weighs 14 oz.

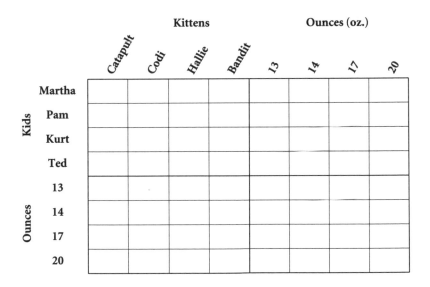

See answers on page 82.

Kurt's Bicycle Ride

Kurt rode his bicycle from Otis Junction, Oregon, to Baltimore, Maryland, in 40 days. He kept a log of the distance between several cities, but he neglected to keep a total. He is curious about the distances he traveled and his averages, but the only map he can find has kilometers only. Can you help? Remember: One mile is equal to 1.6 kilometers.

Days	Distance Between Cities	Kilometers	Miles	Miles per Day (nearest 10th)
7	Otis Junction to Boise, Idaho	838.4		
4	Boise to Ogden, Utah	528.0		
7	Ogden to Cheyenne, Wyoming	713.6		
6	Cheyenne to Omaha, Nebraska	811.2		
2	Omaha to Des Moines, Iowa	217.6		
6	Des Moines to Indianapolis, Indiana	764.8		
8	Indianapolis to Baltimore	939.2		
	Total			

See answers on page 86.

Lily Claire and the Pirates

Team Captain Lily Claire and four other girls on one of two
Pirates teams (varsity and junior varsity) compared their results
from a recent game. See if you can tell how many baskets and free
throws each made, which team each played on, and the total
points for each player.

1. Rachel made three times as many free throws as the player who
   made four baskets.
2. Three players, including the one who made four free throws, are
   on the varsity team.
3. The player who made one basket and no free throws (not
   Teresa), is on the varsity team.
4. Tina made fewer free throws than Teresa, but more than Julie.
5. Teresa, who is on the varsity team, made half as many free
   throws as the player who made twice as many baskets as she
   did.
6. Lily Claire made two more baskets than Rachel, but Rachel
   made two more free throws than Lily Claire.

Players	2-point Baskets					1-point Free Throws					Team		Total
	1	4	5	6	8	0	1	2	4	6	J.V.	Varsity	
Julia													
Lily Claire													
Rachel													
Teresa													
Tina													

See answers on pages 86–87.

Wildcats

Five members of the Wildcats baseball team are listed below, complete with their batting averages and current number of stolen bases. Here are some hints to help you figure out who plays which position and their stats.

1. The catcher, not Billsly or Lewis, has fewer stolen bases than the player batting .309.
2. Lewis's batting average is .20 higher than the shortstop's.
3. The player batting .240 has the most stolen bases.
4. Atkins has fewer stolen bases than Johnston, but neither has three.
5. The center fielder leads in one statistic and is second in the other.
6. Lewis, who hits higher than Billsly and Downey, has stolen seven bases so far this year.
7. Downey, the pitcher, is last in one statistic and next to last in the other.

See answers on page 94.

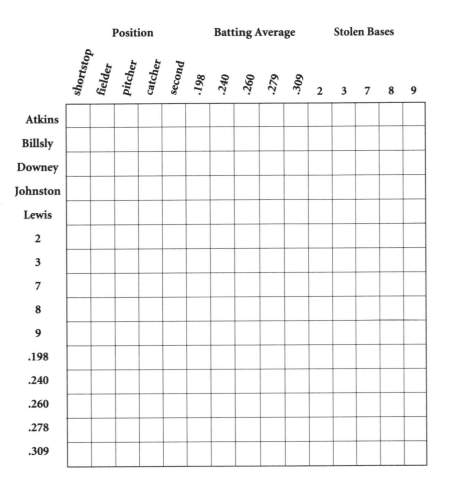

	shortstop	fielder	pitcher	catcher	second	.198	.240	.260	.279	.309	2	3	7	8	9
	Position					Batting Average					Stolen Bases				
Atkins															
Billsly															
Downey															
Johnston															
Lewis															
2															
3															
7															
8															
9															
.198															
.240															
.260															
.278															
.309															

N & G

The five top readers at the middle school are shown in this puzzle. It's your job to figure out how many books each student read, their initials, and their room numbers.

1. B, who is not L, read ¾ as many books as S.
2. G is in Room 103.
3. M read four more books than N and two more than P.
4. L's room is between N's and G's.
5. V read more books than N, who read more than L.
6. The student from Room 104 read eight books fewer than the student in Room 101.
7. T's classroom is 102.

See answers on page 89.

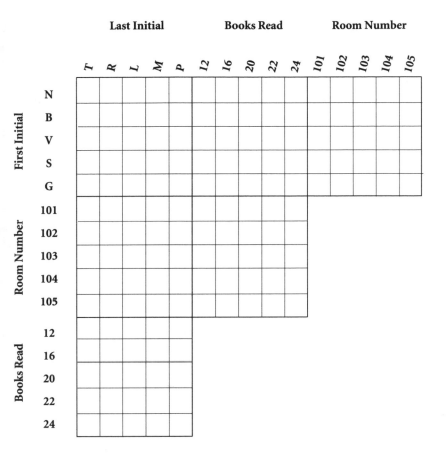

Grandpa Willard's Applesauce

Grandpa Willard says he knows how to make the best applesauce in town. So he's down at Half-Off Dale's Deli telling his pals about it, and pretty soon there's a big argument over which apples and which ingredients make the best applesauce. At one point Dale had to ask them to be quiet because they were scaring off the other customers. So, using the following clues, see if you can tell which apples and which key ingredients go with which grandpa.

1. Cooper hates Northern Spy apples and horseradish.
2. Neither Smith nor Ted would allow lemon in his applesauce.
3. McGee uses twice as many apples as John Willard.
4. Neither Dick nor Cooper likes almond.
5. Neil and Cooper can't stand Granny Smith apples.
6. The one using almond extract, not Rod or McGee, uses 1 lb. apples.
7. Grandpa John uses .5 lb. more apples than Grandpa Frandsen.
8. The grandpa using 2.5 lbs. does not care for cinnamon.
9. The one using three teaspoons of horseradish also uses Northern Spy apples.
10. The grandpa using brown sugar (2 c.) uses 1.5 lbs more apples than the one using Granny Smith apples.
11. Ted and Cooper both disdain Yellow Transparents.
12. Neil likes Northern Spy. He uses three times as many as the one who uses almond.
13. Delicious apples and brown sugar go together, claims Rod.
14. Grandpa Smith uses 4 oz. of flavoring with his Gravenstein sauce, 3 oz. more than Ted.

See answers on page 84.

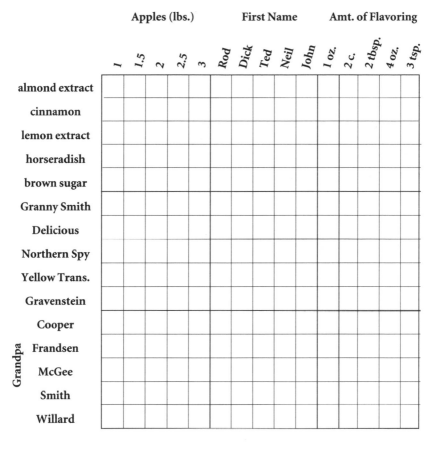

Apples (lbs.)   First Name   Amt. of Flavoring

	1	1.5	2	2.5	3	Rod	Dick	Ted	Neil	John	1 oz.	2 c.	2 tbsp.	4 oz.	3 tsp.
almond extract															
cinnamon															
lemon extract															
horseradish															
brown sugar															
Granny Smith															
Delicious															
Northern Spy															
Yellow Trans.															
Gravenstein															
Cooper															
Frandsen															
McGee															
Smith															
Willard															

Grandpa

Mustardville

It's the town where farmers deliver their hot dog supplies: onions. cucumbers, dill, etc. Determine which driver drives which truck and what he takes to Mustardville.

1. Hiram drove his truck from Pickelton to Mustardville, a total of 32 miles.
2. The cucumber truck is slower than the blue truck.
3. The trip from Relish City to Mustardville, the route of the dill truck, is 4.5 miles. It took the driver 15 minutes.
4. Cucumber Gap to Mustardville is 4 miles.
5. Townes drove the onion truck faster than the red truck.
6. The red truck traveled for two hours.
7. The onion truck drove for 12 minutes.
8. Vance did not drive the blue truck.

	Truck Color			MPH			Freight		
	red	blue	green	16	18	20	dill	onions	cucumbers
Townes									
Hiram									
Vance									
dill									
onions									
cucumbers									
4.5 miles									
32 miles									
4 miles									

See answers on page 88.

Flapdoodle

A Loggerhead Shrike, a Cattle Egret, a Black Oystercatcher, a Red-Breasted Merganser, and a Roseate Spoonbill are in a shouting match over who gets to be first going down the waterslide. They finally take a vote and agree that they will slide in order of height, with the shortest first. Can you figure out who's who and the order of their turns?

1. Jake is five inches shorter than the Cattle Egret.
2. The Loggerhead and Sal combined are as tall as the Spoonbill.
3. Tony gets to go first, the Black Oystercatcher third.
4. Milly is shorter than Willy by 25 inches.

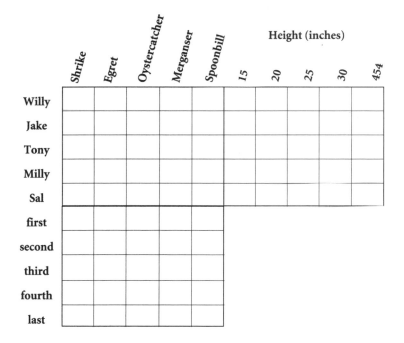

See answers on page 83.

Bone Hunters

Four big dogs went on a bone search. They dug up six bones altogether. One dog found three. Another dog found two. A third dog found one, and one dog found none. You are to help figure out which dog (by name) found how many bones and what breed of dog it is. Good luck.

1. Baggy is the Dalmatian.
2. The dog who found two bones wasn't the Boxer or Muffin.
3. The German Shepherd found more bones than Blue.
4. Muffin isn't the Labrador.
5. The Lab didn't find as many bones as Blue.

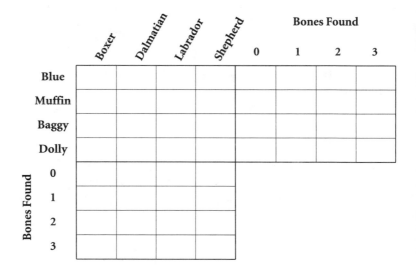

See answers on page 81.

Do the Math

Match the operations in Graphs A and B, do the math, and record the answers in Graph C.

Graph A

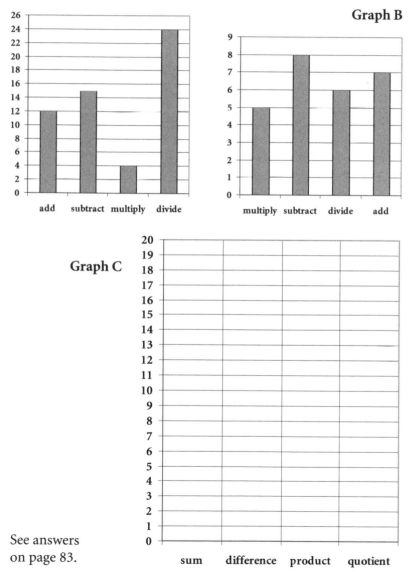

Graph B

Graph C

See answers on page 83.

Nico's Algebra Test

Nico is sure he aced the last algebra test and has the highest average in the class. To give him some much-needed practice, his teacher gave him all the scores and asked him to calculate sums and averages. Columns A to I represent scores on tests taken by Nico and eight of his classmates. Help Nico with the calculations, and match the sum/average of each column to a name. Round averages to the nearest tenth.

1. The person with the highest sum is not Max or Nico.
2. Liz has the lowest average but not the lowest sum.
3. Zane's average of 22.8 is second highest.
4. Ruby's sum/average is in column D or B.
5. Shaw's sum of scores is 149.
6. Nico's sum is nine fewer than Liz's.
7. The highest sum has the highest average, but the lowest sum has an average 1.1 higher than the lowest average.
8. Column G is neither Max nor Moss.
9. Tyne is not B or D.
10. The combined sum for Max and Tyne is 193.

See answers on page 89.

	A	B	C	D	E	F	G	H	I
	11	6	11	2	24	10	17	15	15
	6	9	4	19	26	24	9	13	23
	7	10	13	6	13	26	21	14	5
	4	5	8	14	32	13		16	17
	11	15	3	9	19	32		12	2
	8	1	4	12		44		9	41
	7		7	7				17	9
	2			4				5	19
	3							11	
								6	
								2	
Sum									
Average									
Zane									
Tyne									
Shaw									
Ruby									
Rob									
Nico									
Moss									
Max									
Liz									

Really Exotic Aliens

We are:

Really	Gathered
Exotic	Randomly
Aliens	Outside
Dancing	Uncle
In	Pete's!
Night	
Gowns	:)

Mrs. Tyee's reading group named themselves this year. Can you tell? Despite the weird name they came up with, these students love to read! Figure out how many words per line (average, no rounding necessary) each student in the group read in a recent timed test. Here are some clues to help you solve:

1. Noah read 20 more words than the one who read 11 lines.
2. Stacie read nine lines.
3. Alex read the fewest words.
4. Leah read two more lines than the one who read 108 total words.
5. Dennis read 126 words.
6. Derrick had the lowest average, but read the most lines.

See answers on page 90.

Lines Read   Total Words

	9	10	11	12	14	16	19	84	108	110	114	126	128	130
Leah														
Dennis														
Noah														
Derrick														
Stacie														
Alex														
Ryan														

Average

	9	10	11	12	14	16	19
6							
7							
8							
9							
10							
12							
13							

Saturday Jobs

Mrs. Scatterbones hired four young people to work for her at $10.00 per hour. She needed five things done: wash the car, rake the leaves, weed the garden, trim the hedge, and mow the lawn. Using the following clues, determine who did which jobs (three did more than one job), their last names, how much time it took, and how much each earned.

1. White earned $5.00 trimming and another $5.00 in a different job. Those were her only two jobs.
2. Sarah raked 15 fewer minutes than Gray, who earned the most.
3. The most earned was $17.50, the least $2.50 by Blue.
4. Joey is not Gray.
5. Jered weeded for 15 minutes.
6. Green did three jobs but did not earn the most money.
7. The four worked a total of 270 minutes: 15 washing, 75 trimming, 90 mowing, 75 raking, 15 weeding.
8. Jered and Gray earned $20.00 between them.
9. Green washed the car in 15 minutes. Joey and Sarah trimmed the hedge.
10. It took Green and Kim 90 minutes to mow the lawn. Kim mowed 2/3 of the time.

See answers on page 90.

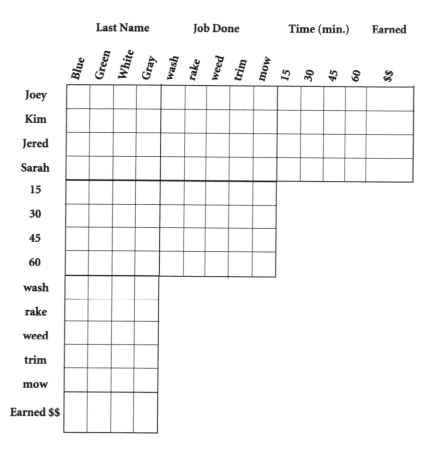

WES Favorites

Mr. Bodle, Mrs. Clark, and Mrs. Olson just surveyed their 3rd graders at Waldport Elementary School to see what some of their favorites might be. The students were asked to list their favorite in each of these three categories: school lunches, holidays, and playground games. Every student voted once in each category.

Use these clues to assist you in determining how many students in each class voted. Also, determine their room numbers.

1. 28 of the students choosing Christmas are from Bodle's and Clark's classes.
2. Five of Mrs. Olson's students chose soccer.
3. Mrs. Clark has just 12 third graders in her ⅔ blended class. 75% of them chose Christmas.
4. 31 of the students selecting pizza are from Mr. Bodle's and Mrs. Olson's classes, not Room 191.
5. ⅓ of Mrs. Clark's students chose soccer.
6. Mrs. Olson has 26 students. Five chose chicken; four, corn dogs.
7. All classes had 2 students choose Thanksgiving.
8. Of the students choosing 4-square, Mr. Bodle had two more than Mrs. Olson, who had 12 more than Mrs. Clark.
9. 3 students from Room 196 chose soccer.

	Room			Favorite Lunch			Favorite Game			Favorite Holiday		
	190	191	196	pizza	chicken	corn dogs	soccer	tetherball	4-Square	Christmas	Halloween	Thanksgiving
Mr. Bodle												
Mrs. Clark												
Mrs. Olson												

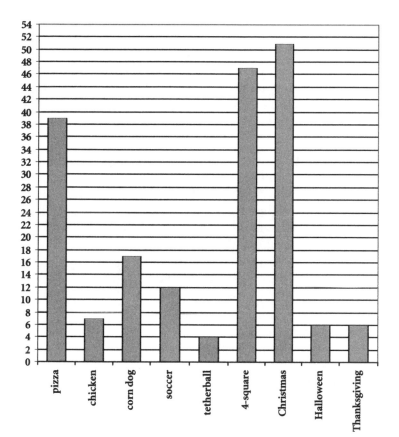

See answers on page 93.

Summer Birthdays

Most of the students attending Heartwood Middle School have birthdays during the school year. For those who don't, they have a special birthday party on the last day of school. This year there are five. Your job is to figure out the five students' birthdays, their full names, and their ages.

1. Iris is younger than Elliott, who was born on August 6th.
2. Avery is older than Ken.
3. Amy, older than Scott and Elliott, has a birthday on the 16th.
4. Ken was born on the 6th.
5. The youngest person was born in June.
6. Wyatt and Eli are the two oldest.
7. Ada and Scott have the first and last birthdays in summer.
8. The student who will be 15 has a July 3rd birthday.
9. The 19th is in August.
10. Eli is 14 when school ends on June 8th.
11. Scott is the youngest.
12. Ken is younger than Amy by just 21 days.

See answers on page 91.

	First Name					Age					Month				
	Ada	Amy	Iris	Eli	Ken	12	13	13	14	15	Jun	Jul	Jul	Aug	Aug
6th															
19th															
16th															
3rd															
31st															
Scott															
Turner															
Wyatt															
Avery															
Elliott															
June															
July															
July															
Aug.															
Aug.															

Traffic Flow

One of the ways the Department of Transportation studies traffic flow is by counting cars in a given stretch of highway during a given time. This particular study counts all the southbound cars from 7:00 to 8:30 a.m., and all the northbound cars from 4:00 to 5:30 p.m., for five days. Your job is to figure out the number of cars going both directions, the average number of cars traveling each day, and the overall averages for the week. Get out your pencils and erasers!

1. The total number of cars counted for the week was 12,200.
2. The total for Tuesday was 2,334, with northbound carrying 264 more.
3. The southbound carried 870 fewer than the northbound for the week.
4. Friday's southbound was 194 more than Tuesday's.
5. Wednesday's northbound count was 83 fewer than Friday's.
6. Thursday's average was 85 less than Tuesday's.
7. Monday's count was 2,606. Northbound had 122 more cars.
8. Thursday's southbound was 147 below average.

	Southbound	Northbound	Total	Average
Monday				
Tuesday				
Wednesday				
Thursday				
Friday				
Total				
Average				

See answers on page 92.

Sweaty Cities

A study of the nation's most sunny cities shows these six as having the most sunny days per year.

Bakersfield, California
El Paso, Texas
Las Vegas, Nevada
Phoenix, Arizona
Sacramento, California
Tucson, Arizona

With just four clues to work with, match the city with the number of cloudless days each enjoys.

1. Phoenix has 16 more sunny days than Tucson.
2. El Paso has four days fewer than an Arizona city, which has four days fewer than one of the California cities.
3. The greatest difference is between a California city and Las Vegas.
4. Fourteen days separate Bakersfield and a city in a different state.

	193	194	198	202	214	216
Bakersfield						
El Paso						
Las Vegas						
Phoenix						
Sacramento						
Tucson						

See answers on page 91.

Soccer Schedule

The Central League soccer season is being planned. The coaches want each of the six teams to play each other team once in the first five games of the season. Help them make a schedule so that this can happen.

1. The Panthers will host the Spartans for the 4th game.
2. The Rockets will play the Bobcats in the 1st game.
3. One of the teams plays four of their games in this order: Panthers, Spartans, Bobcats, Rockets.
4. In the 3rd game, the Panthers will play a team starting with the letter "B".
5. The Buffaloes play the Spartans first.
6. The Cyclones and the Buffaloes meet after the Spartans play the Panthers.

Games

	1st	2nd	3rd	4th	5th
Bobcats					
Rockets					
Panthers					
Cyclones					
Buffaloes					
Spartans					

See answers on page 91.

Slapjack

Two girls and two boys stayed in from recess and played four games of slapjack. Each person won one game (last one in) and each person lost one game (first one out). See if you can figure out who won and lost which games, and the full names of each player.

1. One of the boys lost the first game and won the second game.
2. Jones won a game before Brown, who won a game before he lost one.
3. Mary won before Sam lost.
4. Moore, who isn't Mary, won the game that Lisa lost.

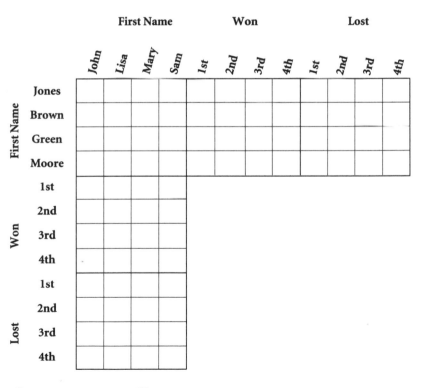

See answers on page 91.

At the Shoulder

The following animals stand anywhere from three feet to over five feet tall at the shoulder. Using the clues, figure out each animal's name and height.

1. Louie is taller than all but two others.
2. Lars is five inches taller than the shortest.
3. The moose is 11 inches taller than Paco.
4. Max is eight inches taller than Milly and 16 inches taller than the llama.
5. Paulo, the shortest, is not a vicuna.
6. The guanaco is exactly the same height as the group average.
7. The antelope is 14 inches taller than the elk.
8. Milly is 11 inches above average, and the reindeer is eight inches under.
9. Sofia is 16 inches taller than the alpaca and 2 inches shorter than Louie.
10. The vicuna is three inches shorter than José.

See answers on page 80.

	Paco	Louie	Sofia	José	Lars	Paulo	Max	Viola	Milly	36"	39"	41"	42"	49"	52"	54"	60"	68"
alpaca																		
antelope																		
argali																		
elk																		
guanaco																		
llama																		
moose																		
reindeer																		
vicuna																		
36"																		
39"																		
41"																		
42"																		
49"																		
52"																		
54"																		
60"																		
68"																		

Flying Wool Ranch

Four ranchers are raising sheep like crazy. And dogs! Using all the clues you can find, match the name of the owners with the ranch each owns, the number of sheep on the ranch, its acreage, and the main dog's name. Oh, yeah, also how much each dog weighs!

1. Clark's ranch has ¹/5 more sheep than the ranch where Joey lives.

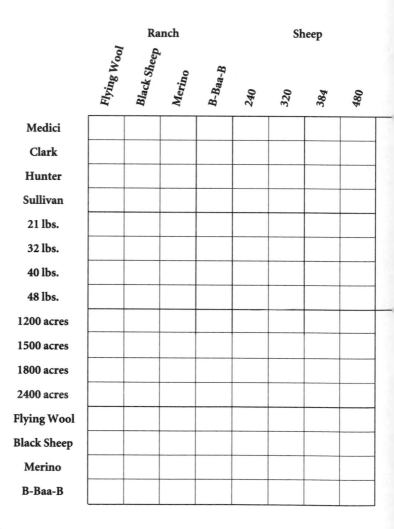

	Ranch				Sheep			
	Flying Wool	Black Sheep	Merino	B-Baa-B	240	320	384	480
Medici								
Clark								
Hunter								
Sullivan								
21 lbs.								
32 lbs.								
40 lbs.								
48 lbs.								
1200 acres								
1500 acres								
1800 acres								
2400 acres								
Flying Wool								
Black Sheep								
Merino								
B-Baa-B								

2. The B-Baa-B ranch has 300 more acres than the Sullivan ranch, but 600 fewer than Clark's.
3. Dingo weighs 11 pounds fewer than the Flying Wool Ranch dog.
4. Medici's acreage is 300 fewer than the Merino Ranch.
5. The heaviest dog, not Skip nor Sullivan's dog, lives on the ranch with the most sheep.
6. The Hunter ranch has ⅓ more sheep than the Merino ranch.
7. Joey weighs ¼ more than Skip, who lives on 2400 acres.

<table>
<tr><td colspan="4">**Dogs**</td><td colspan="4">**Acres**</td></tr>
<tr><td>*Skip*</td><td>*Joey*</td><td>*Blue*</td><td>*Dingo*</td><td>*1200*</td><td>*1500*</td><td>*1800*</td><td>*2400*</td></tr>
</table>

	Skip	Joey	Blue	Dingo	1200	1500	1800	2400

See answers on page 84.

Mrs. Wilcox's Challenge

Mrs. Wilcox, a local recycling center volunteer, challenged four high school classes to see which could recycle the most newspapers in a month, to be judged by weight. The winning class gets milkshakes paid for by the losing class. You have to figure out which class won, the name of the teacher, the room number, and how many pounds of newspaper they each turned in.

1. Room 201 turned in 200 pounds fewer than Mrs. Wilcox's class.
2. Mrs. Lindly's class is on the same floor as the Biology room.
3. Ms. St. John does not teach the English class.
4. Room 210 is the French class.
5. Mrs. Williams's class turned in 200 pounds more than the Biology class and 200 pounds fewer than Room 210.
6. Room 110 buys the milkshakes for the French class.
7. The Algebra class turned in 100 pounds fewer than Room 201.

See answers on page 88.

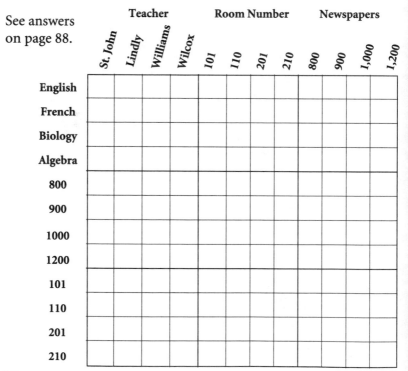

Walking for Wilma

Mrs. Olson's many birds, rats, and frogs are hungry! Even Wilma, her Walking Stick, is eager for more crickets. So some of Mrs. Olson's students decided to organize a fundraiser to buy food for the class menagerie. They got pledges for walking: $2.50 per mile. Using the clues below, figure out how far each person walked, how much each earned, and the total raised. Only the two people who made it all the way walked the same distance.

1. Kim walked 1.5 miles father than Ira.
2. Ian walked 2.5 miles fewer than Luc.
3. Joy walked farther than everyone but two others.
4. Fay walked 4.5 miles farther than Ian.
5. Von went farther than Liv.
6. Eve went .5 fewer miles than Ian.
7. Ada walked 3 miles more than Ira.

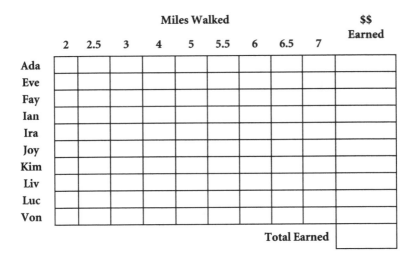

| | Miles Walked | | | | | | | | | $$ Earned |
	2	2.5	3	4	5	5.5	6	6.5	7	
Ada										
Eve										
Fay										
Ian										
Ira										
Joy										
Kim										
Liv										
Luc										
Von										
							Total Earned			

See answers on page 93.

Ten-Pin Alley

"Hey, let's go bowling! You keep score."

Here's how you bowl. You roll a ball down the lane and try to knock over all the pins. There are ten of them.

If you knock them all down with one ball, it's called a **strike**. If you knock them all down in two tries, it's called a **spare**. If you don't knock all ten down with two balls, you count the total number of pins knocked down. You get ten tries (frames) all together.

Here are the scoring rules for bowling:

1. If you knock down a total of nine pins with both balls, for example, you get a score of 9. Seven pins, you earn 7. Six, 6. And so on.
2. If you knock all ten pins down with two balls (**spare**) you earn 10 points *plus* the number of pins you knock down with the next ball.
3. If you knock all ten down with one ball (**strike**) you earn 10 points *plus* the number of pins you knock down with the next *two* balls.
4. Instead of putting each frame's individual score in the corresponding box, you keep a running total.

Sound confusing? Here's an example to help you.

Frame	Ball	Max's Total	
1	first	10	16
	second		
2	first	4	22
	second	2	
3	first	8	31
	second	1	

Now try this. Three people went bowling and here is how each did. Using these numbers, figure out each person's total score.

Frame	Ball	Jeremy's Total		Wynona's Total		Jill's Total	
1	first	10		4		6	
	second			5		4	
2	first	9		7		9	
	second	1		3		0	
3	first	10		10		9	
	second					1	
4	first	8		7		10	
	second	1		3			
5	first	9		7		10	
	second	1		2			
6	first	10		10		9	
	second					0	
7	first	8		9		9	
	second	1		1		1	
8	first	9		6		8	
	second	1		3		2	
9	first	10		8		10	
	second			2			
10	first	8		9		7	
	second	1		0		2	
	Total						

See answers on page 92.

Solutions

At the Shoulder

Louie Elk	54"	Paulo Alpaca	36"
Paco Guanaco	49"	Viola Vicuna	39"
Sofia Llama	52"	Jose Argali	42"
Lars Reindeer	41"	Joe Antelope	68"
Milly Moose	60"		

At the Zoo

The hippo is 12.

The lion is 11.

The otter is 14.

The leopard is 13.

The emu is 10.

Babysitting

Amelia Gray was paid $4.75 per hour, and earned $166.25 for a bicycle.

Bobby Wills was paid $4.50 per hour, and earned $189.00 for clothes.

Carson Jones was paid $5.25 per hour, and earned $99.75 for a computer.

Dylan Sands was paid $4.00 per hour, and earned $190.00 for a trip.

Elvin Ellis was paid $5.00 per hour, and earned $190.00 for college.

Berry Streets Bus

Danny lives on Cherry Avenue and leaves the bus first.

Justin lives on Huckleberry Avenue and leaves the bus second.

Diana lives on Elderberry Road and leaves the bus third.

Bruce lives on Mulberry Street and leaves the bus fourth.

Tracy lives on Blueberry Street and leaves the bus last.

Beverly's Yard Sale

Earned	Leftover	
$6.60	6	
$8.64	3	
$3.72	2.5	
$18.96	11.5	Totals

Bobcats

Name	Height	Average
Aaron Ross	6'3"	14.6
Ben Katz	5'9"	8.0
Dan Blum	6'9"	19.0
Sid Lien	6'0"	4.5
Jon Delg	6'7"	8.8

Bogmen

Billy's Berries	1,200	Bog by the Bay	2,100
Grand Cranberries Ltd.	1,800	Cranberries, Inc.	900
Tiny's Bog Co.	600	Miles o' Bogs	1,500

Bone Hunters

Blue, the Boxer, found 1.
Muffin, the Shepherd, found 3.
Baggy, the Dalmatian, found 2.
Dolly, the Labrador, found 0.

B-r-r-r-r-r

Average temp	−2.4 degrees
Coldest day	2.6 degrees below average
Warmest day	4.4 degrees above average
Closest to average	Sunday
Biggest change	7 degrees
Same three-day temp	−4 degrees
Weekend	colder by 1.5 degrees

Catapult

Martha gets Codi, who weighs 14 oz.
Pam gets Bandit, who weighs 20 oz.
Kurt gets Hallie, who weighs 13 oz.
Ted gets Catapult, who weighs 17 oz.

Check!

Bob wins! Al earned 44.75 points; Bob earned 45 points.

Corn Dogs

Hot dogs	160	Corn dogs	75
Popcorn	40	Pretzels	30
Peanuts	120		

Cornivores

Wombat Willies	11	Body Grabbers	32
Lagoon Slimeballs	44	Lizard Lair	9
Trout School	19		

Dale's Trip

Total gallons	51
Total liters	193.29
Average $ per gallon	$1.93
Miles per gallon	16.94

The Dalton Express

City	Arrive	Depart
Dalton	—	7:15 a.m.
Farmington	7:30 a.m.	7:36 a.m.
Newton	7:51 a.m.	7:57 a.m.
Carroll	9:27 a.m.	9:33 a.m.
Portsmouth	10:48 a.m.	10:54 a.m.
Reedville	11:09 a.m.	11:15 a.m.
Dalton	2:15 p.m.	—

Do the Math

Graph C

Sum	19
Difference	7
Product	20
Quotient	4

Double Bogey

Par	4	5	3	4	4	3	5	4	4	36
Hole	1	2	3	4	5	6	7	8	9	**Total**
Smith	2	5	2	4	3	2	3	4	5	30
Dyment	3	5	5	4	6	3	6	4	3	39
Horn	4	6	4	4	2	5	4	4	6	39
Munro	6	4	3	3	4	4	5	3	4	36

Farmer Bob's Barn

Cats	6
Chickens	10
Cows	4
Goats	8
Horses	2

Five Boxes

A	B	C	D	E
48	4	6	24	10

Flapdoodle

Willy Spoonbill is 45 inches and slides last.
Jake Oystercatcher is 25 inches and slides 3rd.
Tony Shrike is 15 inches and slides 1st.
Milly Merganser is 20 inches and slides 2nd.
Sal Egret is 30 inches and slides 4th.

Flying Wool Ranch

Clark's Flying Wool Ranch, 384 sheep, 32-pound Skip, 2400 acres.
Medici's Black Sheep Ranch, 480 sheep, 48-pound Blue, 1200
  acres.
Sullivan's Merino Ranch, 240 sheep, 21-pound Dingo, 1500 acres.
Hunter's B-Baa-B Ranch, 320 sheep, 40-pound Joey, 1800 acres.

Four Football Fans and Four Pizzas

Peter ate three slices of cheese and one slice of vegetarian.
Bob ate one of each.
Hank ate one of each.
Jason ate one pepperoni slice, two sausage, and one vegetarian.

Fraction Match

G	$3/5$	E	$2/6$
A	$1/4$	—	$3/8$ (circled)
I	$2/7$	B	$4/6$
F	$3/4$	A	$2/8$
H	$7/8$	D	$5/8$
B	$2/3$	C	$2/5$
E	$1/3$	F	$6/8$

Grandpa Willard's Applesauce

Rod Cooper uses:
  2.5 lbs. of Delicious apples and 2 c. of brown sugar.
Ted Frandsen uses:
  1 lb. of Granny Smith apples and 1 oz. of almond extract.
Neil McGee uses:
  3 lbs. of Northern Spy apples and 3 tsp. of horseradish.
Dick Smith uses:
  2 lbs. of Gravenstein apples and 4 oz. of cinnamon.
John Willard uses:
  1.5 lbs. of Yellow Transparent apples and 2 tbsp. of lemon
  extract.

The Great Divide

Jeremy Green took 1 Snickers and 2 Mars.
Derek Jones took 2 Hershey's and 1 Mars.
Jason Smith took 1 Snickers and 2 Hershey's.
Ozzie Tyler took 1 of each.

Half-Off Dale's Deli

Ted had a ham sandwich, ½ soup, and a soft drink for $9.05.
Geri had ½ turkey sandwich, ½ chili, a cinnamon roll, and an espresso for $9.35.
Ginger had ½ a cinnamon roll for $1.20.
Kelsey had ½ beef sandwich, ½ soup, ½ a cinnamon roll, and a soft drink for $7.85.
Tristan had a tuna sandwich, chili, a cinnamon roll, and a soft drink for $11.25.
Beverly had soup, a cinnamon roll, and an espresso for $7.25.
C.J. had ½ a cinnamon roll for $1.20.
Total (paid by Tristan): $47.15

Halloween Party

Emily wore the witch's costume and drank 6 glasses of cider.
Dina won the pumpkin-carving contest and drank 1 glass.
Sam broke the dish and drank 3 glasses.
Donny won the apple-bobbing contest and drank 5 glasses.
Katie helped clean up and drank four glasses.
Erin got sick and drank 2 glasses.

Hogs in a Fog

Chevrolet	24
Dodge	96
Ford	40
GMC	64
Mack	112

Jessica

The oldest, Angela, is 16 years, 4 months.
Ryan is 15 years, 4 months, 3 weeks.
Jessica is 14 years, 11 months, 3 weeks.
Doug is 14 years, 9 months, 3 weeks.
The youngest, Lida is 14 years, 7 months, 1 week.

Kids and Cars

Toyota	5	Chevy	2	VW	2
Dodge	6	Jeep	3	Ford	4

Kookaburra Stew

Augustus, from Wagga Wagga, prefers half a gallon (1.88 liters) of scampi.

Plato, from Gympie, prefers 3 pints (1.41 liters) of perch.

Caesar, from Kangaroo Island, prefers half a pint (.235 liters) of angleworm.

Pluto, from Wollongong, prefers 3 quarts (2.82 liters) of sardines.

Kurt's Bicycle Ride

Km	Miles	MpD
838.4	524	74.9
528.0	330	82.5
713.6	446	63.7
811.2	507	84.5
217.6	136	68
764.8	478	79.7
939.2	587	73.4
Totals	3,008	75.2

Lily Claire and the Pirates

Julia made 1 basket, 0 free throws, played on the varsity team, and scored 2 points.

Lily Claire made 8 baskets, 4 free throws, played on the varsity team, and scored 20 points.

Rachel made 6 baskets, 6 free throws, played on the junior varsity team, and scored 18 points.

Teresa made 4 baskets, 2 free throws, played on the varsity team, and scored 10 points.

Tina made 5 baskets, 1 free throw, played on the junior varsity team, and scored 11 points.

Magazine Drive

1. 142, 302
2. 62
3. December, 147
4. 142, 131
5. 204, 302
6. December
7. 142, October
8. December, 302, 204
9. 302
10. 204, 26, November, 73, December

A Man in a Green Coat

The man in the green coat drove a red motorcycle 48 k. (30 mi.).

The woman with the gold earrings drove a blue sportscar 57.6 k. (36 mi.).

The teen in ski boots drove his dad's green station wagon 43.2 k. (27 mi.).

The old woman in tennis shoes drove a black pickup 55.2 k. (34.5 mi.).

The basketball referee in the fleece jacket drove an SUV 36 k. (22.5 mi.).

Martha's Books

A   48 or 60
B   12 or 24
C   36 or 12
D   24 or 48
E   60 or 36

Misplaced Numbers

Box A   16, 20, 26, 38
Box B   1, 13, 19
Box C   45, 99, 117, 135
Box D   49, 91, 105
Box E   2, 8, 10, 57, 59, 73, 83, 87, 95

Mr. Clark's PE Storage Room

12 basketballs
8 soccer balls
16 softballs
4 footballs
10 tetherballs

Mr. Lockety's New Carpet

Mr. Lockety in Room 186 needs 594 sq. ft. of sage carpet.
Mrs. Ebuley in Room 194 needs 506 sq. ft. of mauve carpet.
Ms. Stalk in Room 168 needs 625 sq. ft. of navy carpet.
Mrs. Eddy in Room 193 needs 552 sq. ft. of taupe carpet.

Mrs. Wilcox's Challenge

Mrs. Wilcox teaches French in Room 210 and collected 1200 pounds.

Mrs. Williams teaches English in Room 201 and collected 1000 pounds.

Ms. St. John teaches Biology in Room 110 and collected 800 pounds.

Mrs. Lindly teaches Algebra in Room 101 and collected 900 pounds.

Mustardville

Townes drove the blue onion truck 20 mph.
Hiram drove the red cucumber truck 16 mph.
Vance drove the green dill truck 18 mph.

My Favorite Class

English	12
PE	25
Social Studies	20
Art	10
Math	5
Biology	8

N & G

NR	20 books	Room 105
BT	12 books	Room 102
VM	24 books	Room 101
SL	16 books	Room 104
GP	22 books	Room 103

Nico's Algebra Test

	Sum	Average
Zane	114	22.8
Tyne	120	10.9
Shaw	149	24.8
Ruby	46	7.7
Rob	47	15.7
Nico	50	7.1
Moss	131	16.4
Max	73	9.1
Liz	59	6.6

Odometer

Curley Lester drove a green car 187.7 miles.
Roberta Fisher drove a red car 181.9 miles.
Danny Delphino drove a black car 186.3 miles.
Rudy Shepard drove a white car 179.4 miles.
Willy Swank drove a tan car 188.5 miles.

Paper Clips

Boxes	A	B	C	D	E	F
	19	16	13	40	55	4

	G	H	I	J	K	L
	22	20	39	26	38	11

Paul's Guppies

Full bowl	15
Rod	8
Heather	4
Nancy	2
Michele	1

Really Exotic Aliens

Name	Lines read	Words	Average
Leah	11	110	10
Dennis	14	126	9
Noah	10	130	13
Derrick	19	114	6
Stacie	9	108	12
Alex	12	84	7
Ryan	16	128	8

Saturday Jobs

Joey Green washed 15, trimmed 45, mowed 30, and earned $15.00.
Kim Gray raked 45, mowed 60, and earned $17.50.
Jered Blue weeded 15 and earned $2.50.
Sarah White raked 30, trimmed 30, and earned $10.00.

Sit-ups

Logan	30	Nicky	10	Chan	15	Dale	120
Leo	60	Zack	5	Axel	45	Andy	40

Slapjack

John Moore won the 2nd game and lost the 1st.
Lisa Green won the 4th game and lost the 2nd.
Mary Jones won the 1st game and lost the 3rd.
Sam Brown won the 3rd game and lost the 4th.

Soccer Schedule

Team	1st	2nd	3rd	4th	5th
Bobcats	Rockets	Panthers	Cyclones	Buffaloes	Spartans
Rockets	Bobcats	Buffaloes	Spartans	Cyclones	Panthers
Panthers	Cyclones	Bobcats	Buffaloes	Spartans	Rockets
Cyclones	Panthers	Spartans	Bobcats	Rockets	Buffaloes
Buffaloes	Spartans	Rockets	Panthers	Bobcats	Cyclones
Spartans	Buffaloes	Cyclones	Rockets	Panthers	Bobcats

Stephanie's Water Bottle

20 ounces

Summer Birthdays

Ada Wyatt will be 14 on August 19th.
Amy Turner will be 13 on July 16th.
Iris Scott will be 12 on June 31st.
Eli Avery will be 15 on July 3rd.
Ken Elliott will be 13 on August 6th.

Sweaty Cities

Bakersfield	202
El Paso	194
Las Vegas	216
Phoenix	214
Sacramento	193
Tucson	198

Ten-Pin Alley

Frame	Jeremy	Wynona	Jill	
1	20	9	19	
2	40	29	28	
3	59	49	48	
4	68	66	77	
5	88	75	96	
6	107	95	105	
7	116	111	123	
8	136	120	143	
9	155	139	162	
10	164	148	171	= Totals

Traffic Flow

	Southbound	Northbound	Total	Average
Monday	1,242	1,364	2,606	1,303
Tuesday	1,035	1,299	2,334	1,167
Wednesday	1,224	1,280	2,504	1,252
Thursday	935	1,229	2,164	1,082
Friday	1,229	1,363	2,592	1,296
Total	5,665	6,535	12,200	
Average	1,133	1,307	2,440	

Vanilla Swirl

Caleb ate 6 scoops of chocolate.
Dakota ate 4 scoops of vanilla swirl.
Joey ate 2 scoops of strawberry.
Sara ate 3 scoops of raspberry.
Loren ate 7 scoops of peach.
Sydney ate 5 scoops of rocky road.

Walking for Wilma

Ada walked 7 and earned $17.50.
Eve walked 2 and earned $5.00.
Fay walked 7 and earned $17.50.
Ian walked 2.5 and earned $6.25.
Ira walked 4 and earned $10.00.
Joy walked 6.5 and earned $16.25.
Kim walked 5.5 and earned $13.75.
Liv walked 3 and earned $7.50.
Luc walked 5 and earned $12.50.
Von walked 6 and earned $15.00.
The total earned was $121.25.

Warm-ups

Penni earned 97 points.
Sam earned 91 points.

Willy earned 104 points.
Jo earned 88 points.

WES Favorites

| | | Favorite Lunch | | | Favorite Game | | | Favorite Holiday | | |
	room #	pizza	chicken	corn dogs	soccer	tetherball	4-square	Christmas	Halloween	Thanksgiving
Bodle	196	14	1	10	3	1	21	19	4	2
Clark	191	8	1	3	4	1	7	9	1	2
Olson	190	17	5	4	5	2	19	23	1	2

Wholesome Decimals

6.09					.878	
.58	5.47	7.997	4.78	3.96	.121	9.25
+.33	+.53	+.003	+.22	+.04	+.001	−.25
7.00	6.00	8.000	5.00	4.00	1.000	8.00

Wildcats

Atkins was catcher, averaged .278, and stole 2 bases.
Billsly was at shortstop, averaged .240, and stole 9 bases.
Downey was pitcher, averaged .198, and stole 3 bases.
Johnston was in center field, averaged .309, and stole 8 bases.
Lewis was at second base, averaged .260, and stole 7 bases.

Woody's Tires

Right front tire: add 12.84 kPa's.
Left front tire: subtract 5.84 kPa's.
Right rear tire: subtract 6.40 kPa's.
Left rear tire: add 45.06 kPa's.
Spare tire subtract 6.74 kPa's.

Puzzle/Skills Chart Index

Title	Skills	Pages
At the Shoulder	Averaging	72–73, 80
At the Zoo	Older than, younger than	4, 80
Babysitting	Dollars per hour	14–15, 80
Berry Streets Bus	Before/after	16, 80
Beverly's Yard Sale	Measurements	10, 81
Bobcats	Averaging	20–21, 81
Bogmen	Fractions	41, 81
Bone Hunters	Compare data	56, 81
B-r-r-r-r-r-r	Graphs/charts	38, 81
Catapult	More than, less than	45, 82
Check!	Fractions/decimals	17, 82
Corn Dogs	Compare data	23, 82
Cornivores	Compare data	5, 82
Dale's Trip	Liters & gallons	25, 82
Dalton Express, The	Time	29, 82
Do the Math	Graphs/charts	57, 83
Double Bogey	Scoring	30, 83
Farmer Bob's Barn	Compare data	39, 83
Five Boxes	Compare data, trial and error	23, 83
Flapdoodle	Taller, shorter	55, 83
Flying Wool Ranch	Fractions	74–75, 84
Four Football Fans and Four Pizzas	Fractions	13, 84
Fraction Match	Fractions	34, 84
Grandpa Willard's Applesauce	Fractions	52–53, 84
Great Divide, The	More than, fewer than	11, 85
Half-Off Dale's Deli	Fractions	36–37, 85
Halloween Party	Compare data	26–27, 85
Hogs in a Fog	Fractions	18, 85
Jessica	Graphs/charts	40, 86
Kids and Cars	Graphs/charts	39, 86
Kookaburra Stew	Liquid measure	42–43, 86
Kurt's Bicycle Ride	Convert kilo to miles	46, 86
Lily Claire and the Pirates	More than	47, 86–87

Title	Skills	Pages
Magazine Drive	Graphs/charts	24, 87
Man in a Green Coat, A	Miles/kilometers	6–7, 87
Martha's Books	Fractions, trial and error	28, 87
Misplaced Numbers	Sorting	22, 88
Mr. Clark's PE Storage Room	Compare data	18, 88
Mr. Lockety's New Carpet	Measurement (square feet)	44, 88
Mrs. Wilcox's Challenge	Heaviest/lightest	76, 88
Mustardville	Miles per hour	54, 88
My Favorite Class	Percent graph	17, 89
N & G	Fractions	50–51, 89
Nico's Algebra Test	Averaging	58–59, 89
Odometer	Decimals	32–33, 89
Paper Clips	Fractions	12, 90
Paul's Guppies	Trial and error	35, 90
Really Exotic Aliens	Averaging	60–61, 90
Saturday Jobs	Dollars per hour	62–63, 90
Sit-ups	Fractions	19, 90
Slapjack	Before/after	71, 91
Soccer Schedule	Organization of data	70, 91
Stephanie's Water Bottle	Fractions	4, 91
Summer Birthdays	Calendar	66–67, 91
Sweaty Cities	Difference	69, 91
Ten-Pin Alley	Scoring	78–79, 92
Traffic Flow	Averaging	68, 92
Vanilla Swirl	Compare data	8–9, 92
Walking for Wilma	Decimals	77, 93
Warm-ups	Graphs/charts	31, 93
WES Favorites	Graphs/charts	64–65, 93
Wholesome Decimals	Decimals	19, 93
Wildcats	Averaging	48–49, 94
Woody's Tires	Convert kPa/psi	41, 94

Also by author Kurt Smith
look for
Math Logic Puzzles (1996)